Make sure that yo **fit properly and ar**

3

It is most important to face in the direction in which you are travelling.

4

It is unwise to attempt to ski if you are not feeling 100% fit.

Never attempt to ski if you feel over-tired.

Extreme care must be taken with ski poles as they can be dangerous if used improperly.

When starting to ski, it is important to learn how to stop yourself properly.

Make certain you understand all signs, and act immediately whenever you come across them.

It is unwise to attempt to cross any road by ski as this can be extremely dangerous.

When putting on skis on a slope, it is essential to fit the downhill ski first.

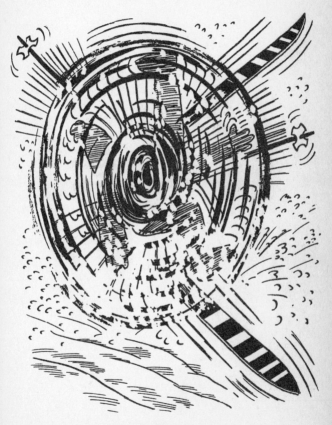

Maps are an essential part of your equipment especially if skiing off-piste.

12

Never go skiing inadequately dressed in uncertain weather. Conditions could get worse.

Except in an emergency, a skier should avoid stopping in the middle of a piste.

It is worthwhile having your eyesight checked prior to your skiing trip.

When turning around on a slope, the best and easiest technique to use is the 'kick-turn'.

If a beginner always keep to the nursery slopes and pistes.

The victim of an accident should only be moved with extreme care, and then only by an expert.

Be prepared for all types of weather conditions whilst skiing.

Never dry ski boots with a fierce heat or with a naked flame.

When learning to ski it is advisable to wear a crash-helmet.

Novices should never attempt to ski where there are rocks or other obvious hazards.

Deep snow skiing is to be avoided by the inexperienced skier.

When skiing off-piste always carry suitable equipment which may help searchers to locate you quickly should you run into trouble.

Do not try and get more passengers than is stipulated in a telecabine or gondola.

Never attempt to ski on one ski if you are inexperienced, as difficulties could arise.

26

It is advisable to maintain your skis and to wax them regularly.

To perfect your skiing practise when and wherever possible.

When deep snow skiing your skis will be below the surface so you must learn to ski by feel, without seeing your skis.

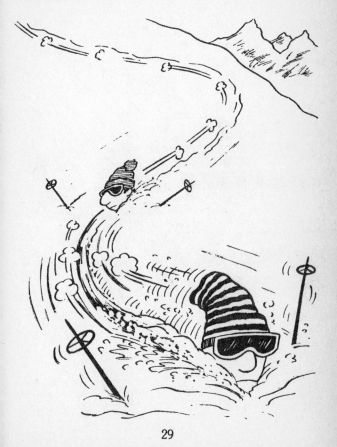

Side-slipping is a technique which allows you to safely descend all types of terrain.

Do not attempt to go onto the slopes after drinking glühwein.

31

Always seek out an expert for any advice.

When going off-piste skiing it is essential to keep a careful watch for hidden dangers.

At all times be courteous and helpful to other skiers.

Make certain that any ski clothes you buy are completely waterproof.

Never put loose skis on the ground as they could set off downhill.

A skier must observe all signs, markers, and especially any instructions from the ski patrol.

Never go off-piste skiing alone.

When overtaking remember to give other skiers a
wide berth.

If you become lost, stay where you are and shout for help.

Do not ski near to any mechanical devices, especially piste-maintenance or snow-making machines.

If possible, try not to ride the T-bar tow alone. It is much easier with another person.

42

Make sure that your ski poles are the right length. An expert will advise you on this.

It is highly dangerous to carry passengers as this can severely restrict the manoeuvrability of the skis.

Whilst waiting for a lift make sure that you keep a proper distance from the next skier in the queue.

Do not practise anything which is too advanced or at which you are unskilled.

46